How To  Save The Planet

10 Simple steps that can change the world

How To Save The Planet

10 Simple steps that can change the world

LUKE EASTWOOD

electric publications

First Published by Electric Publications, 2019
www.electricpublications.com

Text copyright: Luke Eastwood 2019

ISBN: 978-1-5272-4598-3

A CIP catalogue record for this book is available from the
British Library.

Printed and bound on recycled paper in Ireland

Printed by Digital Printing Ireland:
27 Upper Pembroke Street, Dublin 2, D02 X361, Ireland

**50% of the profits from this book
are donated to Greenpeace**

Contents

Acknowledgements 1

Introduction 2

Step 1 – Stop buying stuff you don't need 7

Step 2 – Become flexitarian, vegetarian or vegan 15

Step 3 – Have zero, one or two children 23

Step 4 – Cut down on travel 31

Step 5 – Recycle, repurpose, reuse 39

Step 6 – Cut down on energy use 47

Step 7 – Complain and campaign 55

Step 8 – Plant trees 65

Step 9 – Help clean up 73

Step 10 – Spread the word 81

Checklist 89

Organisations worth supporting 93

Also by Luke Eastwood:

The Journey
The Druid's Primer
Through The Cracks In The Concrete The Wilderness Grows
Kerry Folk Tales
Where The Hazel Falls

www.lukeeastwood.com

Acknowledgements

A big thank you to the publisher and the publishers of my other titles for their support. Special thanks to Joe Eastwood and Elena Danaan for proof-reading the manuscript. Thanks to all my friends and family for their continual support of my work over the years.

Thank you to Greenpeace and all those who campaign for social and environmental justice around the world.

Introduction

If you're reading this you probably are concerned about where the world is going, the fate of humanity and of the planet itself. If you didn't care about these things at all you would not have picked up this book, instead you might be out partying, shopping or some other nihilistic activity that can distract you from the awful truth.

Unless you live in a hole in the ground, you've definitely seen, read or heard about the ecological catastrophe that is fast approaching us; rather like a global bus stuck in top gear, with no brakes, headed for a cliff. We've known for over 50 years that there was a cliff ahead, it started with a few concerned passengers voicing their fears but that collective voice has grown louder and more numerous as the decades have passed.

So, why are we still headed for the cliff? Why has the driver not slammed on the brakes and brought our global bus to an abrupt halt? The reasons for this are numerous and complex but can be broken down into one simple answer – denial. There are many passengers who have a vested interest in the bus keeping going at maximum speed, namely all the money they stand to lose out on if we stop the bus. There's also the fact that very few people want to give up the pursuit of a better life and once they have it, even fewer want to give it up – it's easier to pretend that there's not a problem than confront our wayward behaviour.

As a result of mass denial we have got where we are now – the bus is literally falling to bits before our eyes but is still somehow hurtling towards that cliff at top speed. We can see it happening and we know why it's happening but no-one seems to be able to stop the bus, or get off it. The driver isn't listening, like an automaton he is completely insensible to reason and remains absolutely focused on staying on mission – keep going as fast as possible. To placate the passengers and mollify their increasingly frequent complaints he says "yeah sure", takes his foot off the gas for a few seconds and then presses on regardless.

How can this be happening when nearly all the passengers want to stop the bus? The truth is that the driver has forgotten the passengers, it's almost as if there is no driver and the bus is driving itself, with no fail-safe in place. What this situation needs is for the passengers to stop waiting for the driver to come to his senses, that's not going to happen in time to avoid going over the cliff. What this situation needs is for the passengers to kick the driver out of his seat and stop the bus themselves – there is no other answer to this problem.

Obviously, actually saving this planet from destruction is actually quite different from the simple act of slugging out the driver and taking over this metaphorical bus. However, in reality the steps that are needed to force a change are actually quite simple, it just requires understanding why you are doing it, focused attention on each step and maintaining these actions long term. Sure, it requires making some small sacrifices, but none of these are really that hard to do.

Once you make these changes in your life you'll feel better about our chances and if you can convince some of your friends, colleagues and family to do the same then you really will be making a big difference. Change has to come from each one of us and like all social movements, it starts with a few individuals and spreads like a virus across society. Regardless of your culture, politics or religion, all of these steps are straight-forward to implement, it just requires the will to do it.

Stop the bus, we all need to get off!

Step 1

Stop buying stuff you don't need

Step 1 :
Stop buying stuff you don't need

From early childhood most of us are exposed to advertising – television, radio, magazines, billboards, it's everywhere. Even in poor countries where many can't hope to live a consumer lifestyle people are still exposed to advertising and aspire to be able to one day be wealthy enough to be a consumer.

If the world had an infinite supply of space and resources then perhaps it wouldn't matter so much that we are all brainwashed into wanting to consume, trying to satisfy an urge that actually can never be satisfied no matter how much stuff we buy. Unfortunately the world is not infinite, all the stuff that we buy is made out of metals, chemicals, plastic (from oil), water, wood and fibres all of which come from the Earth. The energy that goes into producing all of this stuff comes mostly from oil, coal, gas, wood and a small amount of renewable sources. All of these materials and the energy to make it comes from the Earth and unlike sunlight, wind and waves (which are virtually perpetual) are limited resources that will eventually run out if we keep piling through them at this incredible rate.

Everyone who makes and sells all our stuff wants us to keep on buying and buying so that they can keep on making and selling more stuff, even if that means the planet gets wrecked. This makes no sense in the long run. As resources become more scarce it gets harder to extract them and more expensive, both financially and in terms of cost to the environment.

Manufacturers aren't going to stop selling their stuff if there is a demand for it, so the only way to stop it is to end the demand. Deep down most of us at some point recognise that all the stuff we own is not what really makes us happy – you can never have enough, that's why millionaires want to be multi-millionaires and multi-millionaires want to become billionaires. Beyond basic security, human relationships, love and friendship are what really make for a happy life – all this stuff doesn't really work for us, it's just taking us all closer to oblivion.

So, take a look at your life, your things. Do you really need another pair of shoes? Do you really need a new television, is the one you have still ok? Do you really need to redecorate the house and change all the furniture? Most of what we buy is not necessary, it's just what we have been conditioned to think that we need in order to feel cool, worthwhile and happy. The price we pay for this is a world that is being ruined by mining for coal, concrete and ores, drilling and fracking for oil and gas, plastic pollution, logging and massive water consumption by industry. We can't hope to bring this to an absolute stop but we can bring it to a crawl tomorrow if we all stop buying incessantly.

For most of human history we've never bought anything at all, for thousands of years we have bartered mostly for essential or useful items, but for the last hundred years we've been increasingly buying items that aren't essential, often aren't useful and only satisfy our vanity and need for self-indulgence. In a hundred years we've turned into consumer zombies!

Humanity has survived, arguably more happily, without consumerism for almost its entire history. We just don't need all this stuff and if we keep on producing and buying all of it *ad infinitum* then we've had it, game over – the planet is doomed!

From now, on every time you feel the need to buy something, ask yourself 'Do I really need this, or is this just my consumer desire?' Probably you don't need more shoes, or a better television or a revamp of the house. Of course when you do need to buy items then you should do so, but give some thought to what are going to be the best options not just for you, but for the impact on the planet. Most of the difference in value and functionality of items is down to perception, the real differences in cost are quite often marginal. If you are going to pay extra for an item it should be because it is made better, will last longer and is kinder to the environment, not because you've been hoodwinked into believing it's worth more.

Have a look through your home and try to identify how much stuff you own that you never or rarely use. You'll probably be shocked how much you already own that you just don't need. Once you get into the habit of not buying stuff it becomes quite liberating – if feels good to no-longer to be at the mercy of the consumer programming we've all given far too much head space to. Save your money and spend it when you need to on the things that are really important to you!

- **Don't buy things you really don't need.**

- **Replace items only when they need to be replaced.**

- **Be selective about what you buy, look for the most ecological options.**

Step 2

Become flexitarian, vegetarian or vegan

Step 2 :
Become flexitarian,
vegetarian or vegan

Meat consumption has been part of human life since our earliest days, the earliest cave pictures show hunting scenes, so clearly it comes naturally to eat meat and our teeth and digestive systems are designed for it. However, we are omnivores, we can survive happily on a wide variety of foods, that does not need to include meat, fish or any animal products.

I love meat and fish, I could happily eat it all day, but I have made a commitment to eat much less of it – once or twice a week is plenty to ensure that I remain healthy, without looking to find alternative sources of some nutrients.

Meat production and consumption is continuing to climb on a worldwide level, particularly in countries like India and China, although it is beginning to decline a little in some western countries. Keeping animals for meat uses huge amounts of resources, livestock needs several times as much land and water to produce meat as it does plant based food. Animals, cows especially, produce huge amounts of methane gas as flatulence (farts) which is far more destructive to the atmosphere than carbon dioxide and is a huge contributor to climate change. Run-off into rivers and seas from the vast quantity of excrement that livestock produces is also causing an enormous pollution problem. Meat production has a massive requirement for water, far more than for growing most crops for human consumption. With water resources already severely stressed in many parts of the world, less meat would mean more available water.

Demand for land to graze cattle and other animals on is one of the biggest drivers of deforestation

– once land is cleared for animals there is no possibility of trees returning, which decreases carbon dioxide capture and decreases production of oxygen that we need in order to stay alive – not a great thing really!

In addition to the negative effect on the climate, the meat and fish industries are responsible for the misery of countless animals that are raised or caught in inhumane conditions in order to maximize profits. Morally repugnant practices are generally well hidden by both the meat industry and the fishing and fish farming industry – they'd prefer the public's mind bubble of a happy existence (prior to arriving on our plates) not to be burst. For many people this alone is sufficient reason to become vegetarian or vegan, however for the rest of us who are perhaps not quite so bothered by the suffering of other living creatures, there is still excellent reason to give up or at least drastically cut back.

Current projections from research suggest that there could be a major food crisis by 2040 if trends in meat consumption do not change in a downward direction. Meat consumption has tripled in the last four decades and the world average continues to rise *per capita* year on year. This is not just because the world population is rising, but because demand is rising as some countries become wealthier and more developed. If everyone were to develop the same demand for meat (about 120kg per person) each year as the USA, there simply would not be enough room on the planet for enough livestock to provide it.

Fish in the oceans could be gone by 2050, according to projections, despite the fact that around half of all fish consumed now comes from fish farming. Humanity is simply removing fish from the sea at such a frantic pace that many species cannot reproduce quickly enough to maintain their populations and some are heading rapidly towards extinction.

Better farming practices on land and in the sea, as well as more responsible fishing will obviously make quite a lot of difference to the impact on the planet, but these changes take time. Time is in short supply – by the time that we wait for governments to change legislation and for industries to implement plans it might already be too late. What will make a difference immediately is if we modify our own buying and eating habits – every person who becomes flexitarian, vegetarian or vegan will be making a valuable contribution towards reducing the stress.

Until recent decades meat and to a lesser extent, fish were luxuries that only the wealthy could afford to eat. Industrialised food production has changed all that but at huge cost to the environment. Ultimately we could eat ourselves into extinction and much of other life on this planet too if we don't change our eating habits! In addition, there are health benefits to be gained from avoiding excessive consumption of meat, dairy and fish. A balanced diet of mostly plant-based foods is far healthier than the meat heavy diets of wealthy westernized nations, that often lead to obesity and other diet related health problems.

There are lots of great alternatives to meat and fish, many of which look and taste very similar – so there is no need for your enjoyment of food to be diminished. Healthy eating does not have to mean being miserable! A very small sacrifice in terms of diet, if enough people join in, will make a huge difference to the damage to the environment, the loss of species and the suffering of billions of animals all over the world.

- Cut down on meat, dairy and fish products.

- Buy free-range or organic meat and fish products that are more ethical.

- Consider giving up eating meat, dairy and fish completely.

Step 3

Have zero, one or two children

Step 3 :
Have zero, one or two children

Population is a very controversial issue. When you start talking about reducing the population some people immediately think of Malthusian conspiracy theories, eugenics, transhumanism, Nazi death camps and forced culling. It's a highly emotive subject and has serious implications for human rights and freedom, so even bringing up the subject can very rapidly land you in hot water!

Back in 1968 Paul and Anne Ehrlich predicted a massive and catastrophic expansion of the world population in their book *The Population Bomb*. They were proven to be quite wrong about mass starvation of humanity due to improvements in agriculture, food production and medicine. However, they did highlight the growing environmental degradation caused by huge population increase and the possibility that if the population kept growing indefinitely it would eventually lead to food insecurity.

Not long after the publication of *The Population Bomb*, in 1970, China introduced a two-child policy, which was replaced by a one-child policy in 1979, although some couples were allowed a second child. This kind of social engineering has been looked on with horror by most of the world because it denies people freedom and choice in how they live. The policy has been extremely effective in China but with the unpleasant side-effect that it has badly skewed the balance between men and women. There are now millions too many men, that have no hope of having a female partner or children (if they want either). The one-child policy was abandoned in 2015 as it was considered no-longer necessary – some 500 million births are predicted to have been prevented. Even with this particularly harsh birth control policy China is still (just about) the most populated country on Earth with a population of about 1.4 billion people, which is still rising, albeit very slowly.

China has made a concerted and unpopular effort to control its rapid expansion in numbers, but in the rest of the world this has not been the case. In much of the wealthy western or westernised nations population growth has stalled or gone into reverse due to massive societal changes, education, contraception and increased prosperity that has led to people having fewer children, without the strong arm of government coercing them to do so.

However, in parts of Asia, Africa, Central and South America, population growth is still galloping along at a great pace. Very soon India will overtake China as the most populated country despite being only a third of the size. Back in the year 1900 the world population is estimated to have been around 1.5 billion people. By 2000 it had risen to around 6 billion people. As I write this (2019) the world population is around 7.7 billion people and still rising significantly, although the rate of growth is gradually slowing. Projections for the future vary enormously depending on how optimistic you are about people reducing the number of children they have. Worst case scenarios indicate there being around 11 billion by 2050, a very conservative estimate would be around 8.5 million, although the United Nations currently predicts it will be around 9.8 billion people.

When I was born (in 1970) there were around 3.5 billion people, in my lifetime the population has doubled, if I make it to 2050 it could have tripled by then! By many estimations we could do with a spare planet to provide all of the resources, including food and water to provide any kind of life for around 10 billion people. Unfortunately, we don't have a spare planet that we can whip out of our pockets to take care of this fast approaching problem. So, where do we go from here? It's all a bit of a mess!

A lot of people don't like to discuss the population issue. Governments don't like to go there either, as forced population controls are deeply unpopular and fill people with fear. Having said that, not talking about the problem of population growth isn't going to make the issue disappear, in fact refusing to acknowledge that it might be one of humanity's biggest challenges guarantees that little or nothing will be done about it.

Optimists say that world population growth will slow down by itself as poor nations become more developed, educated and prosperous because the birth rates drop faster. If that happens then perhaps it's not necessary to do anything, but what if the optimists are wrong? Given past trends, it's likely that we will run into problems unless governments enforce low birth rates or unless people voluntarily choose to have fewer children.

Waiting for governments to act is a non-starter. If they do anything at all it will be too late and will be a belated and horrible curtailing of personal freedoms, like in some dystopian sci-fi movie. If people are really serious about saving this wonderful planet then we need to start making decisions about our families right now. In a perfect world we could all have bucket-loads of children if we wanted to, but that luxury is now gone.

If we want a half-decent world for future generations to live in we need to cut population growth now. I've one child myself and I made a decision a long time ago that I would not have any more, even though I liked the idea of having a sister or brother for my only child.

Surely it's better to have less children and see them living well, than having a small army who will inevitably have a harder life? if everyone does the same thing then we've a real chance to prevent a catastrophe in the future. Saving the world for future generations requires self sacrifice – we all need to play our part in bringing population growth to zero as soon as possible.

- **Have smaller families – it's easier to provide a better life for one or two children.**

- **Use contraception to ensure that unexpected pregnancies don't happen.**

- **Educate your children about population growth and its impact.**

Step 4

Cut down on travel

Step 4 :
Cut down on travel

In the past travelling was a major ordeal; travel on land often required horses which (like people) inevitably get tired, need food, water, rest and sleep. Roads were usually dirt roads and built for travel on foot, horse or carts/carriages. Remote areas had even worse roads or no roads at all and criminals often preyed on travellers who were seen as easy targets. Travelling anywhere on land was arduous and slow before the age of machines so in many instances it was easier to travel large distances by boat – either on a network of canals or by the sea. Travel by sea was often the quickest way to go any significant distance but being at the mercy of (often drunk) sailors and the wind could be unreliable and frequently dangerous.

Everything changed with the industrial revolution, particularly the invention of steam locomotives.

Surprisingly, steam engines were around in Roman Egypt, probably invented by the Greek, Hero of Alexandria in the 1st century CE. Rail transport began even earlier, in the 6th century BCE in ancient Greece, using a paved trackway, powered by men and oxen or horses. Proper railways appeared in the early 16th century in Austria, again powered by humans and animals that pulled a rope via a treadwheel.

Rudimentary steam engines reappeared from the 16th century onwards but it wasn't until the late 18th century that steam engines became mobile, first in ships (Scotland) and slightly later on roads (England). The first fully functional steam-powered railway began in 1804 and the 19th century saw the development of these three forms of steam transport that completely revolutionised travel.

Steam power used coal and like coal power today, was extremely polluting, although the scale of transportation was relatively tiny even at the end of the steam era. The internal combustion engine, using oil based petrol or diesel changed transport even more than rail and steamboat travel, leading to the network of roads and motorways we see today and also travel by aeroplane.

The rapid expansion of transport options and the speed at which journeys could be undertaken must have seemed miraculous and mind-boggling to people during the 19th and early 20th centuries. It has solved a problem that existed for thousands of years and made travel possible anywhere in the world. However, this has not come without a price, as we are finding out now (big sob)! Mechanised transport was always dirty but when it was relatively small scale and there were far fewer people, the consequences didn't seem particularly dire. There was general ignorance about the effects of coal and oil based fuels both on the general environment and on human health –

we know better now and this has been scientifically proven many decades ago.

If coal and oil is so toxic why are we still using it? That's the obvious question and the answer is simple – it's convenient and we haven't come up with any fully viable alternatives quite yet. Electric vehicles are the way forward but even though they don't produce any direct pollution, most of the electricity used to power them is still produced by coal, oil or gas. The production of carbon dioxide and no end of pollutants is still there, but it has been relocated from the vehicle to the power station.

At the moment, large scale transportation such as cargo ships, cruise liners and commercial aeroplanes cannot run on electricity, although some forms of small electric aeroplanes are in development. Currently the two worst forms of transport for polluting the planet are large scale shipping and commercial airlines. Planes require a huge amount of energy to get up in the air and they are only really less polluting (per passenger) than ground based transport for long flights and flights where most of the seats are filled. Another factor is that planes release most of their carbon dioxide and a range of other gases and carbon into the air at high altitudes where it does more damage to the atmosphere. Airplane travel is becoming increasingly popular despite being a major polluter and with no immediate hope of transferring to greener fuel.

Container ships and cruise liners use a particularly dirty form of diesel fuel, which is hugely polluting – one cruise ship can produce the same amount of sulphur dioxide as 13 millions cars in one day! Container ships also produce a lot of pollution from fuel but most people will never see one, yet alone travel on one. As well as air pollution cruise ships produce huge amounts of dirty water, sewage, chemical waste and rubbish. Some companies have promised to use cleaner fuel and try to reduce their enviromental impact but even so, taking a cruise liner is one of the worst things you can do for the planet – sorry I'm such a spoil-sport!

For the time being, travelling any long distances is a dirty business. So it makes sense to cut out or minimise long distance travel – on planes and cruise ship especially. If you can buy an electric or even a hybrid car, this will be far better for the environment in the long term as the technology keeps improving and more renewable energy is coming on line. Hydrogen electric cars may prove to be even better. Car pooling is a great idea, it reduces the impact per person of travel and also helps to reduce road congestion. Taking public transport such as buses and trains further reduces the impact per person, especially as more efficient and non-polluting vehicles are becoming increasingly common.

For short distances it's a great idea to take public transport, a bicycle or even walk. Cycling or walking has great health and fitness benefits apart from having zero emissions! Transportation is one of the biggest polluters of the planet so the more people that change the way they travel, the better it is for everyone.

- **Try to avoid long distance travel as much as possible.**

- **Don't ever take a trip on a cruise liner.**

- **Get a greener electric/hybrid vehicle if you need to buy a car.**

- **Use public transport, cycle or walk more often.**

Step 5

Recycle, repurpose, reuse

Step 5 :
Recycle, repurpose, reuse

People have always generated rubbish and a lot can be found out about previous civilizations by archaelogists through looking through ancient rubbish – yuck! Depending on the climatic conditions, stone, pottery and metal can survive for thousands of years but generally speaking most organic materials will break down very quickly.

Traditionally people have disposed of their rubbish away from their homes, perhaps on the edge of their village or buried in pits and this has worked well for thousands of years. This was all well and good before the invention of plastics – a material that can take anything from fifty to many thousands of years to decompose. What happens with plastics generally is that they just break up into smaller and smaller pieces without decomposing – it remains in the environment for a very, very long time, with unknown long-term effects.

We've only had plastics for a very short period of human history. The first experiments with natural polymers, such as rubber, began in the mid 19th century and the first synthetic plastic was created in 1839 but not rediscovered until the 20th century. Plastics such as Parkinsine and PVC were invented in the late 19th century but it wasn't until around the beginning of the 20th century that man-made plastics began to be practically and commercially viable. Since then production and use of plastics has grown almost exponentially – from about 1.5 million tonnes in 1950 to about 322 million tonnes in 2015. Production of plastic has been predicted by experts to increase by 40% by 2030, which means that the problems we have right now are likely to become much worse, especially as only 10% of plastic makes it into the recycling process. We're all very much aware of what a huge pollution problem plastic is causing, especially in the world's oceans, but there is actually 4 times as much plastic in the soil on land, much of which will remain there for hundreds or thousands of years.

Obviously, producing less plastic should be our goal and manufacturers should be obliged to convert to biodegradeable plastics as soon as possible. However, part of the problem is the poor uptake of recycling, both from a domestic and industrial point of view. Not enough people and organisations are seriously committed to recycling plastics and other recyclable materials such as metals, glass and wood products. This needs to change in a big way, but even more important is the massive upscaling of the recycling industry in order to deal with all our recycling. At the moment a huge proportion of what is sent for recycling never makes it through the process and ends up being dumped in land-fill or is burned in incinerators.

Obviously ordinary people cannot recycle materials but we can repurpose and reuse more than we currently do, whilst also demanding that government and industry rapidly develop recycling facilities to cope with increasing demand for recycling. In the past it came naturally for people to repurpose and reuse items rather than just throw them away – we were broke! The disposable culture of today, with built in obsolescence of many items would have been unthinkable to most people only fifty years ago. When I was a child most mechanical or electrical items were expected to last for decades and would be repaired until their useful life was over. Items of clothing were repaired instead of being thrown out and glass bottles were returned for reuse by manufacturers.

Largely because of economic necessity, as well as a more long-term attitude to our possessions, waste was kept to a minimum and items were looked after and maintained for as long as it was possible to do so – this is a way of living that we desperately need to get back to. Many items can be given a new life as something else after they no longer serve their original purpose. Some interesting, if not nutty, examples are a sofa made out of an old bathtub or walls made out of old tyres or old glass bottles. There are countless items that can be repurposed and many that can be used again – such as a reusable water bottle or coffee cup that you can refill thousands of times instead of wasting money and plastic on disposable water bottles and cups.

Clearly we can't recycle, repurpose or reuse everything in our lives, but with a little bit of thought we can reduce our rubbish significantly and at the same time save ourselves a lot of money in the process. Hopefully recycling facilities will soon catch up with the demand for recycling, but in the meantime you should use recycling collection or bring it to recycling depots anyway. If enough people ask governments to continue expanding recycling schemes as well then it is likely to happen faster.

- **Try to avoid buying plastic – look for alternatives in other materials.**

- **Recycle as much of your rubbish as you possibly can.**

- **If possible find another use for things you want to throw out or give them to someone who can make use of them.**

- **Reuse items instead of buying single use products – e.g. cups and bottles that can be reused for years.**

Step 6

Cut down on energy use

Step 6 :
Cut down on energy use

Humans discovered harnessing energy other than our own a long time ago. The first form of energy that man learned to use is fire. Opinions differ regarding when exactly humans began to be able to control fire anything from 1.5 million years ago in Africa, 800,000 years ago in Israel or 350,000 years ago, also in Israel. All these dates fall within the Lower Paleolithic period, or what is more commonly called the early stone age and it would have been a recent ancestor of modern humans such as *Homo erectus* that learned to harness fire. Fire had many early uses apart from keeping warm and cooking – clearing land, hardening wooden tools, heat treating stones, scaring animals away, heating clay for containers as well as acting as a meeting place and beacons.

Much later on humans learned the next step in harnessing energy, which was the use of other animals. It's generally thought that humans first domesticated animals around 15,000 to 12,000 years ago, starting with selective breeding of wolves to produce dogs, including highly useful Pugs and Chihuahuas. From about 10,000 years ago sheep, pigs and cattle were beginning to be domesticated while the horse came much later, around 6,000 years ago. Around this time period it is thought that people first started using animals for transport, first with sledges, perhaps pulled by dogs (not Chihuahuas I hope), and later with wheeled carts or wagons pulled by oxen or horses.

After learning to harness the energy of animals humans began to harness the wind, starting with sailing around 5000 years ago in Egypt. It took a long time to progress to the first windmills, which appeared first in Persia around 500BCE and had developed into vertical shafted grain mills by about 1,300 years ago. By the end of the 1st millenium CE wind technology was being developed in Mediterranean Europe and in China.

Use of water power appears to have come somewhat later than wind power, but when exactly is not clear. Mesopotamian records refer to irrigation machines although there are no specific details about how they were used. The first known water wheel was developed in Egypt around the 4th century BCE with similar developments arriving soon after in India, Greece and China.

The concept of renewable energy was completely unknown to people in ancient times, they made use of animal, wind and water power because that is all that was available. All this changed with the industrial revolution and the development of commercially viable steam power, gas, coal and electricity, which effectively began the demise of renewable energy. Steam power (from burning coal) became viable towards the end of the 18th century and began to gradually replace wind power in shipping. It also began to replace water and wind powered machines, especially once steam engines became mobile.

Gas power, was initially created from coal, wood or oil, through heating it in a low oxygen environment. This was first commercialised in Britain in 1785 to provide lighting for street lights and houses. Manufactured gas quickly became popular in Europe and America in the 19th century and also became used for heating systems and cooking. Gas lighting gradually declined in popularity with the development of electric light in the 1870s, which didn't involve explosions quite so often! Discovery of natural gas supplies in the 1890s meant that gas eventually no longer needed to be manufactured and it became increasingly used for heating, cooking and for electricity generation.

Electricity, although probably discovered in ancient Mesopotamia for electro-plating, wasn't again explored until the 1600s and electricity generation wasn't developed until 1831. Amazingly the first electric car was built in America in 1835 by Thomas Davenport, but it was far too costly to be practical. Although the first commercial alternating current system was hydro-electric, the majority of electricity generation has come from coal with gas and oil also extensively used even now.

Coal, oil and gas seemed like the answer to all our energy problems – a seemingly endless supply of energy rich fuels that can be made mobile and provide heat, light, transportation and electricity. Of course, we now know that none of the fossil fuels are ever lasting – if we keep using them at currently expanding rates, we could be in big trouble by 2050. Not only is fossil fuel in limited supply but it is horrendously polluting the whole planet, poisoning the land, air, water and affecting all life. We've known about the enviromental impact for over a hundred years but commercial interests and a formerly low population meant that it was easy to ignore the growing downside of readily available fossil fuel energy.

Recent predictions are that it is possible to have 100% renewable energy worldwide by 2050 if we rapidly speed up implementation. Ironically it means going back to newer forms of the technologies that were invented a long time ago – windmills, water power, electric cars as well as completely new inventions such as solar and biothermal power! In the meantime we all need to do what we can to reduce our own energy consumption.

This means moving away from coal, oil and gas power in our everyday lives by transitioning to electric heating, electric cars, lower energy lights and devices. If we can cut down on our overall energy consumption by switching off car engines, lights and devices, turning down heating or AC when not needed then this will help reduce the burden on the planet. The future of environmentally friendly energy is undoubtedly electricity - we can also help by switching our electricity supplier to one that uses all or primarily wind and water power. Green energy is coming, but while it ramps up, cutting our own energy consumption as much as we can is absolutely vital for our future.

- **Move away from dirty energy – ditch coal, oil and gas energy as soon as possible.**

- **Switch to a renewable energy electricity supplier.**

- **Find ways to cut your own energy consumption through better efficiency and using less (also saving you money long-term).**

Step 7

Complain and campaign

Step 7 :
Complain and campaign

It's more than likely that cave people sat around the camp fire complaining about situations in their lives, just as people do today. It seems to be very much part of human nature to complain about something, even when there's very little to complain about! Complaining to friends and family is all well and good and getting something 'off your chest' might well help you to feel better, although in many instances it doesn't change the reality of your situation one bit.

Apart from making you feel a little better, complaining doesn't change anything unless you go about it in the right way and direct it where it is going to have some impact. Throughout history people all over the world have struggled to have their complaints dealt with and be treated in a respectful and just manner. The oldest recorded complaint is written down in cuneiform script from Akkadian Mesopotamia, probably around 1750BCE. It was written by a disgruntled businessman in the city of Ur, complaining about rudeness and the poor quality of copper he had bought from a supplier.

This is rather a trivial example, but it shows that individuals have been well able to articulately complain about situations they don't like for thousands of years. In truth complaining is often the only way to bring about social change, both for individuals and entire groups of people. Complaining is the first stage of resistance to any unacceptable situation, although this has often led on to violence and wars historically, it is the precursor to any form of social change.

Slavery has been an appalling scourge upon mankind for thousands of years, but only due to public pressure was this disgusting lucratrive trade made illegal. Unfortunately it still continues illegally and secretly in many countries. Civil rights for African Americans and other minorities (such as Native Americans) would never have been obtained if huge numbers of people had not complained and campaigned at the instigation of Martin Luther King Jr. and his colleagues.

Equality for women has been a long and hard fought battle, some limited suffrage for women was achieved in Sweden in 1718. This was long before the suffragette movement of Europe and America in the mid 19th century, started by Elizabeth Cady Stanton, had gained any traction. Campaigning for equal rights for women continues around the world as the situation varies enormously from one region to another – Saudia Arabia only gave women the right to vote in 2015 and the right to drive in late 2017!

Freedom for India, and subsequently for all countries within the British Empire might never have happened were it not for Mohandas Gandhi's non-violent campaign of resistance. India's success inspired countless others around the world and helped bring to an end all the European empires and make imperialism unacceptable. In South Africa a small group led by Nelson Mandela led to a mass movement and the eventual dismantling of the evil racial segregation of Apartheid.

Countless social movements throughout history have been started or led by one or two individuals that eventually inspired huge numbers to protest and campaign for change. The *status quo* does not change without application of huge energy to overcome the inevitable resistance to a comfortable and advantageous situation for powerful groups. However, sometimes change is both necessary and inevitable, it just takes a catalyst to get the process started.

Back in 1992 a 12 year old Canadian girl gave an impassioned speech at the UN Conference on Climate Change in Rio de Janeiro in Brazil. She was hopeful and her heart-felt pleas affected many people, although it didn't translate into much positive action on the part of governments, businesses or people generally. Twenty years later that same girl - Severn Cullis-Suzuki returned to Rio and gave another impassioned, although less well publicised speech on the environment.

Ms. Cullis-Suzuki, who is still an enviromental activist, concluded that not nearly enough had really changed and that it was pointless to sit around waiting for governments and businesses to wake up and do something to safeguard the future of coming generations and the planet generally. I've come to the same conclusion myself, which is why I have written this book and I'm hoping that you reading this will make you do the same.

Greta Thunberg, became world famous in autumn of 2018 after starting a one person strike in protest against climate change in Sweden. In many ways she is the successor of Cullis-Suzuki, although she came to a similar understanding of the reality of our situation at the tender age of 15. Thunberg's Friday strikes at the Swedish parliament have inspired a movement amongst school children all over the world, leading to about 1.5 million school children protesting in March 2019 for action against climate change. In additon to protesting she has made a personal commitment and convinced her family to do likewise by giving up plane travel and becoming vegan.

While she has been nominated for a Nobel Peace Prize and been showered with awards, Greta Thunberg realizes that platitudes don't change anything, it's action that is needed. Children, like her, have a far more limited ability to effect change in the world than adults, who have far more freedom (yippee!). Yet despite this, she has galvanized millions of young people to join her in demanding action from governments and commercial organisations.

Obviously most of us who may be inspired by Thunberg and others like her, will not get publicity and recognition, but what does that matter? We need to take action first in our own lives to save the planet and also apply as much pressure as possible on those who have the capacity to make wholesale changes. Hopefully, Thunberg has kick-started a movement that will revolutionize human society and bring a halt to the tsunami of environmental destruction that is upon us. Reading about it in the paper or watching it on television is NOT ENOUGH, it requires personal involvement from all of us – and that means you!

- Write to your politicians and companies demanding radical policy changes.

- Boycott unethical businesses and unethical products.

- Join protests in your village, town or city or start one.

- Support campaigners such as Greenpeace and Friends Of The Earth financially, in local groups, with petitions and on social media.

Step 8

Plant trees

Step 8 :
Plant trees

Trees have played an important part in the history of the Earth, in the ancient past they had a major part in oxygenating the atmosphere to make it breathable for animal life. We still depend on them to create more oxygen. It's widely held that the asteroid impact at Chicxulub in Mexico, some 66 million years ago wiped out the dinosaurs but it also wiped out much of the plant life that existed at the time. The impact itself wasn't the main problem – the long period of darkness caused by the debris blocking the sun caused a plummet in temperatures and stopped all plants from photosynthesizing.

This was the last of 5 great extinctions that have occurred in Earth's history, the worst being the Permian extinction of 251 million years ago that left only 4% of species remaining. All of life here day is descended from that 4%. Periodically smaller scale disasters have been caused, mostly by huge volcanic explosions, like that of Mount Tambora in the Indian ocean, which errupted in April 1815. This is less famous than the erruption of Krakatoa in 1886, but was actually far worse, causing a global lack of sunlight in 1816, known as the year of no summer. This was not long enough to cause mass extinctions but it did cause massive crop failures and famine all over the world.

Even with these catastrophic events, trees and other plant life have always quickly recovered and spread all over the planet. Trees have also been affected by periodic ice ages, going into retreat during expansion of glaciers but again they have always returned, quickly recolonising the Earth. Some scientists say that we are entering a 6th extinction event now, in the Holocene era, but this time it is being caused by humans and not random events.

We are now realising that trees as well as ocean plankton play a vital role in regulating the climate of the planet and the balance between the carbon dioxide that they breath and the oxygen that we humans breath. Since the last ice age ended, about 12,000 years ago, humans began to spread back into the more northerly and southerly areas along with other species. Since the stone age people have made axes, but originally they would not have been any good to chop down anything more than a tree of a few years old.

As people multipied and became more sophisticated, with the move from hunter gatherers to farmers, axes also improved from about 3500BCE onwards, meaning that we could cut big trees and make use of them. It's estimated that since that time we have chopped down over 55% of the Earth's trees, even though there are an estimated 3 trillion left today. The rate of tree cutting has dramatically increased over time, which today is around 15 billion a year and still rising (which sucks!), but tree felling was already a significant problem in ancient times.

The *Epic of Gilgamesh*, the world's oldest known book, describes the felling of the forest in what is now modern Iraq nearly 5000 years ago. This area of the Middle East generally was full of forests and is now pretty much desert due to a warmer climate, to some extent, but mostly due to humans. Ancient civilisations did a great job of denuding the environment of trees and replacing them with grazing animals such as cattle, sheep and goats, which prevent new trees from growing back (thanks a bunch for that!).

The Babylonians, Egyptians, Greeks and Romans all stripped their own countries of most of their trees that they needed particularly for smelting metals as well as for construction and fuel. The Greeks and later the Romans were forced to import wood from other lands around the Mediterranean and beyond, denuding those countries too. In the medieval period, tree loss continued across Europe, India and China as populations expanded and demand for wood increased. By the time of the European colonial powers, demand for wood for ships for the empires of Portugal, Spain, Britain and Venice meant that wood had to be imported from northern Europe and Ireland. With the discovery of the New World, empires had a new vast area to exploit as well as southern Asia as more European countries began colonisation.

So here we are now, with the tropical forests of South America and Asia still disappearing at an alarming rate, despite dire warnings from all over the world. The boreal forest of the northern hemisphere is the world's largest, stretching across Canada, Scandinavia and Russia but this too is being rapidly exploited by loggers. We know well that deforestation leads to soil loss, flooding, species loss and eventual desertification but we haven't stopped yet or even slowed down significantly. Some reafforestation efforts in Europe and China have been very successful at regenerating land and reintroducing biodiversity, but so far it has been way too small to make any real difference.

With over 7 billion people on the planet it would make a big difference if every one of us could plant at least one tree - that would be 7 billion new trees right away! Obviously, the real answer is to stop the logging industry in its tracks and roll out a huge replanting programme all over the world. If we keep on chopping trees faster than we replant them it will lead to a huge biodiversity disaster as well as having an effect on ocean acidification. Without trees we'd be totally reliant on ocean plankton to generate oxygen and if increasing ocean acidification kills them off then we will be looking at a short future, gasping for breath (not great really)! Reforesting the planet could not be more vital.

- **Plant as many trees as you can – even if it's in a container pot.**

- **Educate your children about trees and encourage them to plant and look after them.**

- **Support organisations that are protecting trees and involved in reafforestation.**

- **Boycott companies that have a record of deforestation.**

Step 9

Help clean up

Step 9 :
Help clean up

Human beings have always been messy. Apart from creating rubbish we've been affecting the environment more severely since we began moving away from a nomadic, hunter-gatherer lifestyle. As soon as we began to congregrate in large groups, the beginnings of urban life we have polluted our local environment. By the end of the 4th century BCE the city of Rome had already developed a serious water problem. The river Tiber, the primary source of fresh water supplying Rome, had become badly polluted due to human sewage (eeewww)! The Romans got around this problem not by being more careful with their crap but by building an aquaduct. Since all their rubbish, including excrement and waste water fed into the sewer system, went straight into the Tiber the problem was only going to worsen. As the city expanded more aquaducts were added, with 10 being built by the 3rd century CE.

In the past many of our pollution problems were temporary rather than chronic and also fairly localised. As we've become more numerous short-term pollution has become chronic and the spread of pollution has reached a far greater extent as we have swallowed up most of the formerly wild and unpopulated areas of the world. The days of moving to somewhere else to begin polluting again are long gone, in fact we are currently polluting largely uninhabitable but pristine areas for resource extraction.

The answer is simple – produce less pollution, but as we try to cut down on the level of pollutants being created and deposited in the world we also need to try to clean up the previous pollution and the pollution that we are adding to the world every day.

Much of the previous pollution we cannot do much about as individuals, apart from campaign for governments and companies to go and clean up the mess that is still there. This mess varies enormously from toxic lakes permanently contaminated with heavy metals, landfills that are full of historical rubbish, much of which is toxic and most worrying – radioactive material sites.

The biological mechanisms of the planet will break down virtually all of our pollution given enough time, even after terrible disasters such as oil spills, but we are currently polluting the air, sea and land faster than the planet can repair the damage. The most dangerous and long lasting pollution of all is nuclear waste, which has been steadily increasing since World War II.

Nuclear power seemed like a great idea that would solve all of our energy problems but the truth is that radioactive isotopes produced by nuclear power can be dangerous for thousands of years. Radioactive material is currently stored on site or in remote locations in containers but even the containers themselves become contaminated. With no way to permanently store radioactive waste, metal or concrete vessels eventually degrade meaning that leaking into the environment is guaranteed at some stage. After the disasters of Chernobyl and Fukushima there should have been a moratorium on nuclear power but incredibly the industry continues to expand around the world, with no solutions for safe disposal of the ever-increasing stockpile of dangerous waste – great stuff!

As individuals we can campaign for an end to nuclear power and diversion of investment into renewables instead. We can also campaign for phasing out dirty power from coal, fracking, tar-sands, oil and gas generally. We can also campaign for far greater punishments for large scale pollution caused by businesses – who are responsible for far more of it than the general population. Beyond that we can make personal efforts to clean up some of the pollution that is all around us. This might involve small things like taking a bin bag out with you when you go for a walk to the beach, in the countryside, or even in a park. Although technically it's is the responsibility of local government to clean up the environment, in practice it's just not getting done properly. If each of us made picking up rubbish a regular effort it would reduce the amount of pollution in the environment, including that which ends up buried in the soil, in our rivers and in the sea.

In addition to this we can personally make a commitment to avoid putting contaminants into the land and water as much as possible by stopping using pesticides such as weed killer in our gardens. We can also refrain from using artificial fertilizers and use only organic, eco-friendly ones. If we switch from using petrol and oil based machines – everything from cars to lawnmowers, this will help reduce pollution of the air, soil and water. Ideally we'd switch to ecofriendly paints to decorate our homes and offices and when we do have to use toxic paint make sure to take the cans to recycling depots where they can be processed safely.

Tidy towns is an idea that is taking off in many countries, this is an encouraging group effort that can be sociable as well as helping to clean up communities. Even if you aren't able to actively take part, you can help support them financially. Reporting littering and dumping to authorities is also very helpful as well as verbally confronting individuals (assholes) who insist on doing so. While embarrassment is not going to stop all people from this shameful behaviour, it will cause some to stop and think about their actions.

Although individual action alone is not going to solve the problem of cleaning up it will make a big difference and continued pressure on government and business will eventually force them to act responsibly.

- **Campaign for government an**

.

- **Campaign for closure of the nuclear industry and long-term nuclear waste planning.**

- **Join a tidy towns group or set one up in your area.**

- **Make a personal effort to clean up your local environment.**

- **Phase out personal use of polluting chemicals in your life.**

Step 10

Spread the word

Step 10 :
Spread the word

Making a difference as an individual can seem daunting. At the very beginnings of every social movement the instigators always feel isolated and alone, possibly desperate and unconfident about the likelihood of success. As we all know, great social movements of the past have 'snowballed' sometimes very quicky, causing a significant shift of consciousness among the population as a whole.

Quite quickly, what was acceptable behaviour a short time ago becomes widely unacceptable today and into the future. This is what humanity needs to achieve and pretty damn fast. This book is intended to play its part in that process by inspiring you, the reader, to make some serious changes in your lifestyle and behaviour. You don't necessarily need to do every single step, if you even just take on board half of them then that is a step in the right direction. What would be a disaster would be for you to just put this book down when you finish it, forget all about it and just carry on with living your life, business as usual.

Of all the steps in this book, step 10 is the most important. One person or five people is going to make negligible difference to the future of the planet. It is for this reason that many concerned people don't bother to do anything – because one person alone can't make any significant change. This fatalistic apathy is exactly what corporations and corrupt governments are relying on to keep things as they are for as long as possible, even though they know that this is suicidal in the long run.

Doing nothing isn't really an option, but more than that, we all need to encourage and convince each other that this is worth doing, that we can make a difference – together. One person can inspire another and that person someone else and so on. In this way one person becomes several, several becomes hundreds, hundreds become thousands and eventually millions or even billions. Two perfect examples of this are how religion and technology have spread. Many of the world's religions were begun or inspired by a single person, such as Gautama Siddhartha, Muhammad, Jesus of Nazareth, Zoroaster and many others. In each instance their followers started out as barely a handful but in quite a short time they mushroomed to thousands, becoming billions in some cases today.

The same is true of technology, although in many cases it has taken much longer to transfer than religion. The wheel was seemingly invented in ancient Sumeria but spread far beyond that region, eventually becoming so common-place hat people took it for granted. The same can be said of writing, cooking, agriculture, modes of transport, building and a whole host of techniques for living that most people don't even think about any more because they are so ingrained. The changes we all need to make may seem new and strange at the moment but if these become the norm very quickly they will completely lose their novelty and strangeness.

The first thing you can do is remind yourself of your personal commitment to follow most or all of the steps I've outlined. With so many distractions from the media and all our modern daily responsibilities it's so easy to forget about many things that we consider important. Cut out or copy the list on the following pages and pin it on your notice board, stick it onto your fridge or some other place where you will see it regularly. By doing this it will become a daily reminder to your overstretched brain of what you can do

practically to make a change. There's also a li
of major organisations that are fighting hard t
save the planet, join them and support them i
this fight.

The next thing to do is to tell other people abou
what you are doing, lend or give them this boo
and ask them to read it and pass it on. Hopefull
your friends, family and colleagues will take o
board some or all of the steps and tell their ow
circle of people around them too. This is ho
social change happens – person by person unt
enough people buy into it to give it unstoppabl
momentum.

If ever humanity needed a grassroots change, thi
is it. Other social movements have made a hug
difference to equality and the quality of life fo
millions of people, but the state of the environmen
on our planet directly affects the future of ever
single living person and those not even born yet

f we can't play a part in bringing about a major hift in lifestyle and taking responsibility then we eally don't deserve things to go better for us. We eally don't have much choice if we want the bus o stop driving over the cliff – there's no time to ose, don't wait for everyone else to do it, get up and do it yourself!

- **Put up your list to remind you of the steps you're taking.**

- **Tell other people about what you are doing.**

- **Give or lend this book to anyone willing to read it, ask them to pass it on.**

Step 1 – Stop buying stuff you don't need

Don't buy things you really don't need.

Replace items only when they need to be replaced.

Be selective about what you buy, look for the most ecological options.

Step 2 - Become flexitarian, vegetarian or vegan

Cut down on meat, dairy and fish products.

Buy free-range or organic meat and fish products that are more ethical.

Consider giving up eating meat, dairy and fish completely.

Step 3 – Have zero, one or two children

Have smaller families – it's easier to provide a better life for one or two children.

Use contraception to prevent unexpected pregnancies.

Educate your children about population growth and its impact.

Step 4 – Cut down on travel

Try to avoid long distance travel as much as possible.

Don't ever take a trip on a cruise liner.

Get a greener electric/hybrid vehicle if you buy a car.

Use public transport, cycle or walk more often.

Step 5 – Recycle, repurpose, reuse

Avoid buying plastic, look for alternatives in other materials.

Recycle as much of your rubbish as you possibly can.

If possible find another use for things you want to throw out or give them to someone who can make use of them.

Reuse items instead of buying single use products – e.g. cups and bottles that can be reused for years.

Step 6 – Cut down on energy use

Move away from dirty energy – ditch coal, oil and gas energy as soon as possible.

Switch to a renewable energy electricity supplier.
Find ways to cut your own energy consumption through better efficiency and using less (also saving you money long-term).

tep 7 – Complain and campaign
Write to your politicians and companies demanding radical policy changes.
Boycott unethical businesses and unethical products.
Join protests in your village, town or city or start one.
Support campaigners such as Greenpeace and Friends Of The Earth financially, in local groups, with petitions & social media.

tep 8 – Plant trees
Plant as many trees as you can, even if it's in a container pot.
Educate your children about trees and encourage them to plant and look after them.
Support organisations that are protecting trees and involved in reafforestation.
Boycott companies that have a record of deforestation.

tep 9 – Help clean up
Campaign for government and industry to clean up pollution.
Campaign for closure of the nuclear industry and long-term nuclear waste planning.
Join a tidy towns group or set one up in your area.
Make a personal effort to clean up your local environment.
Phase out personal use of polluting chemicals in your life.

tep 10 – Spread the word
Put up your list to remind you of the steps you're taking.
Tell other people about what you are doing.
Give or lend this book to anyone willing to read it, ask them to pass it on.

Organisations worth supporting

Greenpeace
Greenpeace International, Ottho Heldringstraat 5, 1066 AZ
Amsterdam, Netherlands
Tel: +31 20 718 2000 Fax: +31 20 718 2002
Website: greenpeace.org

Friends of the Earth
Friends of the Earth International, Secretariat, P.O.Box 19199,
1000 GD Amsterdam, Netherlands
Tel: +31 (0)20 6221369 Fax: +31 20 639 2181
Website: foei.org

Extinction Rebellion
International website: xrebellion.org

Deep Green Resistance
Deep Green Resistance, PO Box 112, Moab, UT 84532, USA
Tel: +1 206 395 6251
Website: deepgreenresistance.org

World Wildlife Fund
WWF International, Av. du Mont-Blanc 1196 Gland,
Switzerland
Tel: +41 22 364 91 11   Website: worldwildlife.org

One Tree Planted
One Tree Planted, 145 Pine Haven Shores Rd #1000D,
Shelburne, Vermont, 05482, USA
Tel +1 800 408 7850 Website: onetreeplanted.org

Ecosia (search engine company that plants trees)
Ecosia GmbH, Schinkestraße 9, 12047 Berlin, Germany
Website: ecosia.org